Looking BACK... Moving FORWARD

BYARUHANGA SOLOMON

ISBN 978-1-0980-6387-0 (paperback)
ISBN 978-1-0980-6388-7 (digital)

Christian Faith Publishing, Inc.
832 Park Avenue
Meadville, PA 16335
www.christianfaithpublishing.com

Printed in the United States of America

I dedicate this book to my children, *Kevin*, *Mercy*, and *Tanya*. I wasn't always there for you to read you bedtime stories or to play with you because of life's challenges. At some point, I felt I wasn't the best example of a father to you, but I want you to know that nothing fills my heart than the love and thoughts I have for you. I love you all so much. I believe someday I will make it up to you for the lost time I missed with you. You have a lot ahead of you to look to. Every step you take, every experience you make, take it as important as the goal you want to reach, for your step determines how far you can go and speaks to whether you have what it takes to make it in life. I believe in you, my children. You have got what it takes. Always remember these words:

- Live your life with integrity.
- Love people and avoid being selfish.
- Let God come first in all you do; He will always guide you. He lives in you. You just have to listen to that positive silent voice in your heart; He is always speaking.
- Read the Bible and pray, for God manifests Himself in His word. His word creates the world around you. It's you who choose the kind of world you want. He can do the impossible if you believe in His word.
- Family comes first.

- Get married before you have kids. Marriage brings respect and favor to your life. You become a mister or a missus.
- Look for your blood. When you find where you belong, it's like a kingdom.
- Refuse to be alone. You belong to a great lineage.
- Avoid walking in pride. Live a humble life.
- Be bold and courageous.
- Be confident in yourself. You can do all things and anything you put your mind or hands to when you focus. You can become whoever you want to become. Believe in yourself whether with the wrong or right decisions. Therein lies the testimonies that make you victorious.
- Be consistent in all you choose to do. One step at a time, you will get to where you want to go. Success belongs to you.

Preface

Am I a student of life?

Life in its simplicity reveals that you know where you have come from, where you are, and where you want to be. Whatever you want to become, life puts you in one position or another. This book is just meant for you, looking back and moving forward. We all often get caught up in life-shifting gears, which tend to bring a major change in our lives. Gears are meant to shift. In other words, they will reduce or speed up an automobile. It is in the nature for human beings to be on the move. Never are we in one place. We keep shifting from one place to another, from here to there. Our life is…but…a clock (ticktack).

Before you choose to move forward, taking that step or decision, you must look back for you to appreciate what lies ahead of you. In my book, I talk about my real-life stories and stories of people I have had a personal encounter with, true-life stories, relationships, reality, and life in itself that will help you look at life in a different perspective before you make certain moves, decisions, or judgments. You will realize that you might need to check yourself and grab hold of those things that have been detrimental and life-choking in your past on the one hand and then the future you desire on the other hand. You get to a point where you must weigh your own life; and believe me, you want the best results for your life, for nobody wants to live a life of regrets, and neither do you.

In every platform, be it good or bad, when you look back, choose to learn from all life experiences. Every experience is a piece of your life. You have to figure things out before you move forward. Learn from the past to be stronger in the future. Always look at the brighter side of life. I hope this book opens a new meaning to your life and to those you share it with.

Acknowledgments

With a lot of sincerity and humility, I want to express my heartfelt gratitude to the special people who have helped me make this life worth living and a reality. Life is real, and the people who have been there all the way give it purpose. I want to thank my children, who gave me a meaning to live. Since I had my first child, that was when I realized that I now had a reason to live. *Kevin*, *Mercy*, and *Tanya*, that special place for all of you in my life can never be replaced. Children of my youth!

A big thank you to the Rubaga Miracle Center Cathedral family for giving me an opportunity to know Christ and to grow in my Christian life. It was here that I gave my life to Jesus, and my life's purpose is revealed each day of my life. I will forever be grateful. I will forever be thankful and grateful to my pastor, *Robert Kayanja*, for being a father to me when I needed one. Being a minister in my home church in my youthful age was the best thing that happened to me as a young man. I was blessed to be able to serve in my home church, a place where I had life-changing experiences and memories.

My youth pastor was *Martin Wampamba*, who was a friend and a big brother who accepted me as stubborn as I was and believed in me even when I doubted myself. Through him, many youths with outstanding talents were able to express themselves, and among them was a dance group that I happened to be a part of that emerged and caused a dance revolution in the country. At that time, many young people turned to Christ, seeing and knowing that it's okay to dance in church too, and it caused tremendous growth in our church. And many of the dancers have become great ministers and leaders. He led the youth by example. From him I learned to pray even when my prayer didn't make sense to me. I kept praying as I saw God love me and change my life and bless me at the same time.

A big thank you to my brother Clifford, who has always been an encouragement even when I was a mess. He stood as a brother to me. And now he gets the message out of my mess. Now he believes that God cares just because God never gave up on me even when I got to my worst as a youth. Emma, my other brother, played a big role in my writing of this book. When I first wrote my book and I told him about it, he asked if he could read through, and his feedback pushed me to go ahead as he kept asking me how far I had gone with the book.

I have been writing this book for over twenty years, but I kept on losing my material. I however did not give up. I kept starting over and over again.

Emma was a smart child whom any parent would be proud of, turning out to be the best student in the country in his high school and in college during his youthful years. This earned him a great deal. He being who he is and what he has become and accomplished in life is an inspiration to me. Yet the sky is the limit. I call him a barrier breaker. It's always good to surround yourself with people who see value and believe in you.

A special thank you to a family that took me in and loved me as their own and took good care of me when I needed a family. They gave me a bed to sleep on, food to eat, and everything I needed in times of need and took good care of my princess (Mercy). A lady by the name of Alex Kayizzi and her entire family. My family will forever be grateful.

Claudia Belak, who is an amazing lady and baby nurse from Tirol, Austria, and a dear friend of mine, who was there for me and my family too. She was always a blessing and a person who will always be special to my family.

Precious Proscovia Namazzi, my dear special friend who happens to be a registered nurse—her name says it all. A person who believed in me and taught me to always have faith and to have a positive mindset—such a caring and loving lady. If I could, I would have put a picture. She always has a smiling face, and she has a joyous persona with too much positive energy that drove away my negativity. I can never express how much gratitude I have for all that you have done for me. I am blessed to have met you as my friend. Thank you, precious.

Centa Terry and the entire family from the International Church of Las Vegas. The family that captured my heart with lots of love and welcomed me in their home in Vegas and blessed my life. Three days in their home was a lifetime experience of God' grace and goodness. Josh, Joey, Mr. Terry, and Mandy! Meeting you was a blessing.

George Timothy Lubega, a.k.a. *Exodus*, one of Uganda's finest gospel artists, a true friend and a brother of mine—you blessed my life.

Ivan Akansima, now you have no idea, but watching how God has been faithful to you in all ways was always life inspiring. Being able to stand strong, focused, and committed and staying a loyal friend, you blessed my life in a special way and always have been an encouraging and uplifting voice in my life. This generation awaits to hear the goodness of God in your life.

When I look back at all the people whom God has used to touch my life, I am forever grateful to God. If God didn't lead them, I wouldn't have moved another step in my life. May God reward you all. May you have great success in all you do.

Insight

In life, we all want to move forward, not just in personal issues—to you it might be business, politics—you name it. The only way you are going to have different results is when you look back, not to stay, but to clean up your mind and freshen yourself up for your journey.

I want you to take a moment and look back at your life, specifically at what was not done right, what failed you, who wronged you, what you missed, why your family rejected you, what business deal flopped. It is probably going to bring back memories that might be hurtful, but remember, it is just a past! Before you hate again or give up, look at yourself back then and recall. Well, if you are honest enough with yourself, you will realize that for the most part, you had a lot to do with it.

The point is, what do you learn from those memories? Whatever you pick from your reflection will either equip you or fail you. Notice that I am not talking about you failing, but rather about you knowing why you failed and what failed you and essentially moving on.

The only way you can move forward in life is by looking back at your mistakes and making things right or learning from those mistakes so that you do not make the same mistakes in the future.

Your future has a lot to do with your past. You might not have had the chance to determine your past, but you have a choice to turn your life around, as well as those of people around you; use it wisely. It matters with what attitude you are reflecting on your past.

I am somebody.

Having grown up in a muddled or dramatic family, as a young man, I suffered a lot of consequences. I experienced so much trauma that my childhood is something I never enjoyed at all. I have no good childhood memories. I grew up in a family that never cared about my existence. A life with my sisters, brothers, father, and "stepmother" for a few years that triggered me to search for a life worth living—a life worth telling.

Having been raised in a home where I was referred to as a bustard as my second name, I felt that home was not the best place to be, most especially when the place you thought was home is the very place where you carry signs of abandonment, forgottenness, abuse, neglect, rejection—you name it. Now as a young man, growing up with such a load in my heart, by the time I was eighteen years of age, I felt like I was forty-five, seeing that I had by then become an expert in handling stress just because I grew up in such an environment that made my life miserable at that time. However, I held on to faith, believing that there was a better life even when I was denied education by my own father, for I had dropped out of school for over seven years.

After a few years of tears, hurt, and misery, there was a dim light flashing in my heart that made me feel like life would be better someday. My experience was really dramatic. I remember times when I was being kicked out of my father's house, spending many days and nights on the balcony, alone in the cold, scared to death for my life, wishing my mother was around. Unfortunately, my sweet mother was in such an unstable state that she could not be of help to me, and most people were blind to me as well. I seemed invisible to everybody, but thank God I still lived through it all.

I still remember the days and nights I starved without anything in my stomach. I was almost left to die of hunger by my own family. Such circumstances made me look at life as not worth living. I always felt so lonely, forcefully isolated by my own, which had left a serious effect on my life in that I often found myself doing whatever I do alone. I had this fear of facing rejection, and so most times I found it hard to give in to anybody. I happened to have lost a lot of good friends because I had a fear of getting hurt and probably vice versa.

Well, we all go through stuff, right? But I have come to realize that although life gets to be so hectic most times, we can choose to make it better. You can choose to walk through any of life's challenges as a better or worse person. Even though I went through such hardships, I found a treasure that turned my life around. I discovered I am not what people called me then; I am not a bustard! No way! I realized that those who treated me badly were just but a small number compared with the unknown who could welcome me in their arms and receive and accept me.

My deceased stepmom—may her should rest in peace—used to tell me that I would never make it in life, that I would never amount up to anything. At first, her words seemed to have such an impact on my life to the point of me dropping out of school because of lack of tuition and never being provided for by my father. Life was a mess because I took her words. Her sounds sounded so loud in every step I took, until they were silenced by destiny. There was a silent but rather powerful voice that mentioned of a person within me who is greater than he who is in this world. That was an awakening of faith within me. A leaping for joy and hope within me like it was a dawning of a brand-new day with great expectation of an amazing unknown.

What people say against or about you should not determine whom you turn out to be but rather what you take in. That may heavily determine what you become. After people have called you all sorts of names, whom do you call yourself? What do you say of yourself? Do you even know who you are? Whatever answer you have is a result of what voices you choose to listen to or words you take in. I, however, hope you choose to listen to a positive voice that says good things about you next time because whatever you listen to is stored in your heart, and out of the abundance of your heart, the mouth will speak.

I have come to realize that depending on how we are raised, situations may push us to the wall, and we could start to believe that we can never make it in life. Unfortunately, this has affected many people all over the world. I, however, strongly believe that we can make a difference. Let us choose to make the world a better place. You might not have chosen the way you were raised, but you can choose the way you want to live your life starting today. I choose to live right, and I choose to live a life that one may look up to and be inspired to appreciate life.

Have you ever asked yourself these questions? Who admires me? Or why would somebody be attracted to me? If you still have a problem with answering these questions, then you have to do something about yourself. Do a soul self-check. Look at yourself in the mirror, and let your soul search your inner self for answers. I bet you will not give false evidence about yourself. But above all, whatever you investigate about yourself, let it be a lead to a clue about who you really are and what you are, and let the right judgment about you bring a revelation of faith and hope about your life ahead.

I used to judge people who I thought did not like me, thinking they were so full of themselves and wondering who they thought they were; and a voice would tell me, *Not everybody is supposed to be your friend.* Associating with people doesn't qualify you as their friend. Friends will choose you just like you choose who should be your friend. People confiding in you doesn't make you friends. Others are just comrades; you happen to do things for the same cause. When it's all said and done, they will leave. The fact that a person doesn't know you does not justify that he doesn't know who they are.

When you know who you are, you don't have to announce your arrival on any occasion. What has made you become who you are will make room for you. People will always identify you with what you have made of yourself! But seek not to be known; rather, live a life of integrity and consistently work on being the best at what you do. Then God will introduce you, for He makes all things beautiful in His time. See! It's easy to become a celebrity; what in fact do you celebrate? Know who you are and live right to do what is right! Fight for peace, equality, gender balance, children's rights, and human rights. Live to help somebody else. That, to me, is the definition of living right. You are somebody being waited upon; reveal and release the hidden treasures in you.

Being a father is a sole purpose of every man. But to be called dad, It has to be earned through a built relationship

Every individual has a different upbringing. Life does not go easy on many people while growing up, and that is what it was for me. It was not easy, but that was my pathway, my life process, and I embraced it regardless. I talk a bit about my father, with all due respect, not to attack or disrespect him, but the fact is he was not there for me when I needed him as a child. And what I went through growing up was hard for me as a child, and that really hurt a whole lot—the fact that I had a father who totally ignored my existence all my life. I mean, we all want to be loved and shown love. All I know about my dad is what I can narrate from my experiences. But I got to hear from one of his old friends that while growing up, my dad was a great guy; he was a sportsman, a great footballer (soccer player). I also learned that he loved music a lot, which is no coincidence that I have a heart and ear for music, although I never got the chance to experience that firsthand. It's unfortunate that I never experienced that good side of him. However, hearing all the person he was to others sometimes makes me smile and get to be thankful of the little truth I got to hear.

I always had this longing, wishing we shared a few good experiences, but that didn't happen to me—no fishing with Dad or teaching me how to ride a bicycle or how to treat a lady or how to be a man. Otherwise, it got me thinking that something must have happened in his life that changed him into the person he had become, but somewhere within me, I believe my dad could have been a great guy, although I can't very much testify to that! I say all of these because I missed a father's experience, him being absent from his position.

If you are a father reading this, I implore you to talk to your children and be their friend while being a parent. Love them and tell them you love them because it matters to them! All my life, I have missed out on love from my dad; and I can tell you, life was not easy for me to a point of envying people who always dined, laugh, or play with their children. If you are a man, never forget that children need you at every stage of their upbringing. Try to be there for them with or without money. All they need is you. Be there to support your children mentally, emotionally, and financially.

Friends could not give me the love I needed! Whatever relationship I happened to be in, I never felt enough love or care just because I knew not how to respond to it. At some point, I lost my self-esteem and confidence, I lost my pride as a child, and I always felt neglected in whatever society I associated with. As heartbreaking as it is, nobody ever wishes their child to go through such. Let's live to fight child neglect at all costs. It's an all-humans responsibility.

Make it a point to spend some time with your children and just love on them. Do not be too busy to talk to your children. Well, you work hard to make sure they get whatever they deserve, but without showing them your love and giving them your time, you will have a negative impact on their lives and destiny. As a parent, you have the power to change that, and it's never too late to start. Start from when you received awareness of your absence in your children's lives.

It's easy to be a father, but to be called dad, you need to earn it. You must be there for your children to call you dad. I am looking forward to taking my dad out the same day with my brother, just for fun, and talking about how we can start afresh and hug as one. I need to do that someday. If you have been a victim like me, don't hold on to hard feelings—allow your heart to soften and let go of the old stuff, and allow yourself to see a new day, a new beginning. After all, they are human like you, bound to mess at any time. But we all deserve a second, third, and fourth chance to make things better; and in my next book, I will tell you how it all transpired.

If you have issues with your parents, you must work it out to win them back. Do not wait for them to beg for your forgiveness. The fact is few parents would do that, and others simply won't, for you are still but a child to them. Only God can humble a parent. They are your parents. Know your place as a child. Sow your seeds according to the expectation of the harvest. We all want a good fruit.

She Is Not Just a Stepmom; She Is Your Family

Many young people, based on their personal experiences, say that stepparents are not family, and their defensive attitude keeps both parties out of the other's life. As a child, you are affected, and your stepmom's attitude will be affected as well.

The fact is, it's not that comfortable when someone new joins the family, but before you crucify your mom or dad, think about them. The reason why people make certain choices is to make life a better place for them and those around them. You might have a stepparent in your home today, and they might not be your blood relative, but if they have the same beliefs as you do, and they are doing their best to nurture you. Give them a chance! In due time, you will realize they are truly a part of your family.

If you have a bad experience with a stepparent, choose to learn from their mistakes and make yourself a better person in society. Many will appreciate your positive contribution to the community. However, that can only happen if you choose to learn how to forgive. Your future is greater than your past; you've got to pave the way.

If you are a stepmother, I urge you to love those children you call your stepchildren like your own. Remember, someday you will have your own, or you already have your own! How would you want them to be treated? Start now and sow that seed of love! Act like you have come to join the family and not to tear it apart. Choose to feel loved and needed. Feel at home and keep a positive mind. You can make those children love you too if you treat them like your own, and it's possible for them to love you beyond your expectations. Love covers a multitude of sins.

Country Experience (Village Experience)

As a family, we happened to have a chunk of land on which lies our ancestral site, which was approximately 4.5 square miles, which later disappeared because few seemed to have seen its value or appreciated how it got to be acquired and/or, to put it into perspective, the sacrifice made by my late uncle. However, I always enjoyed going up-country with my family since we could go once in a long while for holidays to see our grannies. But a new norm as to why we had to go to our ancestral home changed this time. My father organized a trip for me and my brother Cliff, and this is how it unfolded: Usually, it took us one hour and a half to get to the village, so we embarked on the journey.

When we reached the village, we received a warm welcome but however, that lasted a day; then things changed. The next morning, we had to wake up by six o'clock in the morning to walk five kilometers through the bushes to get to a coffee plantation, where we had to work and clear the fields for the next three weeks. I wasn't ready for that! My father loved farming, and this time, he had brought us as machinery. We had to work from 6:30 a.m. to midday and then walk again for five kilometers back to the house. We did that job for two weeks, and we were done. I was fourteen by then. Cliff was seventeen, and my other brother was thirteen. Good for him, he was used to life in the village, so it wasn't so hard for him. But it was still child labor.

requested to sleep in being underage. Nobody wanted to take responsibility in case something went wrong with me.

I spent almost three months of sleepless nights on my father's porch in the cold breeze with mosquitoes feeding on me, and nobody cared whether I slept there. It looked like everybody had become blind to me, for they had gotten used to my suffering. To my surprise, I never got sick, not even a single day in all the nights and months I slept in the cold. God protected me. It was so mind-boggling to be neglected by my own that I couldn't take the rejection anymore, so I had to find an option that I can never forget. I had nowhere to go, and after I had failed to find an option, I came across an abandoned madman's crib, which I happened to occupy for sixty nights. Now this was a space between bushes beside a football pitch in the neighborhood near my high school. I remember my dramatic drills every morning, where I would jump out of the bush like I had been jogging since it was next to a football pitch with my sleepy, unwashed face. I don't know why, but I always thought nobody could ever discover my little secret, until after a while, some people who woke up early for work started looking at me suspiciously, wondering why a child was always jumping out of that bush every morning. So I changed the time I exited my crib. I learned what time the early risers passed by, and I would always come out before they passed by.

I always felt so ashamed, but after some time, I got used to the criticism because it had almost become my only place of refuge. So I stopped caring about what anybody said or thought of me. After all, nobody ever offered me any help. After a while, I resorted to a different option. It's funny but true. I would visit some people in the neighborhood, but I would spend the day dozing off in the compound chairs the whole day on an empty stomach. By that time, the story had run around the neighborhood that I had run away from home and refused to go to school. A few people had the right judgment about me being a runaway from home. And since I was just a child, they always thought I was being the stubborn kind, so I was ignored. Most people thought I was being a naughty kid.

But it was a false story. I wasn't wanted in my father's house. I was just but a child neglected, but now am a grown man. I'm big

We embarked on many other projects, such as planting three acres of tomatoes, cabbage, cassava, maize (corn)—altogether we were looking at over ten acres' worth of crops planted. And in all this, my father always promised that we now had worked for our school fees, but that wasn't true. Whenever we were harvesting, he would say our school fees would come from the next harvest, and we kept on waiting until everything was harvested, and we had missed out, delaying our return to school. However, I have some good memories from these experiences: the fact that I got to learn to do some farming and to spend some time with my grannies forcefully.

Through all these empty promises, as stubborn as I was, I started being naughty too, and he always turned to anger. He would create another project with another promise (lie). That was when I realized I was trapped, and at some point, I got so sick and he never seemed to care. He always asked whether I was strong enough to go back to work. We had a maize mill on the compound, so he asked me to work there as I gained my strength to get back to the plantation, and I did until I couldn't take it anymore. I made a few bucks from the maize mill, and I boarded back to the town center. I was sixteen by then.

You Can't Fight Yourself

At some point, I always said I would never be like my father. I did not even want anybody to tell me I resembled him. But guess what, the more I fought him, the more he manifested in me, and that was so not good. After ten years of not wanting to be like my father, I find this guy and he tells me, I remind him of my dad! What? Did he just say that? Well, he did! Since then, I realized I wasn't fighting him but fighting myself! On that point, most times parents mean well, however hard they are on their children, and the children take it the wrong way because communication between the child and the parent is missing. I missed ten years of learning that those ten years turned into years of fighting myself. That's a lot of time wasted! I wish it was spent on trying to make somebody of myself then.

I realized it was up to me to decide what to take or what to leave behind of my childhood experiences. Although I do not have any good childhood memories, I still choose to let it stay behind me. I choose to learn from my father's mistakes and to look at the few good moments I happen to remember about him. If you want to be a good student of life, you need to make wise decisions and carefully make your choices. It will always help you not to make the same mistakes that your predecessors made. Whenever faced with an experience, sit your mind down to learn through that experience. Most times, experiences speak of your future potential. Learn to face your fears.

Respect and Honor Your Parents

We are all human, and we are not perfect. We all make mistakes. Y parents may not have been there for you, but you do exist becau of them. They are the reason that you are and responsible for yo existence. If you only knew what they went through to bring you up then you will realize their role in your life.

Since I had just run away from the village, I had nowhere to go, and so I just went to my father's house. Thank God that the only communication we had those days was always through letter writing. You would give a taxi driver the letter, and when he got to the destination, somebody would ride a bicycle to take it. So it could take at least two to three days, so I knew I would clean up in those few days before my father was contacted.

After about three days, I heard that my dad was coming back home, and he didn't want to find me in his house. He was a very tough and scary man. He tortured me (I will never treat my son like he treated me). I promised myself that I had to be a good dad. Now that I am a man of age, I do know what it is to discipline a child and to abuse a child, for I was abused.

Before he got back, I had to run away from home, not knowing where to go or whom to run to, which made me end up moving around the neighborhood during the day. And in the night, I would look for shelters where to put my head down, and that didn't always end up so well because I would be chased away from all places I

enough to know the truth by now. I was rejected by my own father. Till today, I don't know why my father never dared to care or love me! I was a smart, hardworking, and very respectful kid. I only became stubborn to survive. I don't know why, but it is not a good thing for you parents to bring your past grudges and dump them on your children. Children end up being victims of circumstances and paying for consequences they don't even know about. I started to think that probably I was just a victim of circumstances, for I hadn't done any wrong to deserve being mistreated. As a parent, please clear your mess and let not your children pay for your sins.

My First Love "Nisha"

While I was writing all this, memories of somebody who was, and still is, special came back and this person was my first love. The reason why I am obliged to make her a part of my journey is that she knew me, and she loved me for me; she was there for me. Whenever she was given pocket money for school, she knew I was hustling, so she would share whatever she had! She was my first love, and I believe she was the most beautiful young lady who ever crossed my eyes. She almost left me blind, for after her, it took me ages to see anybody else. We met in 1997. She was a friend indeed!

I always thought I would never need anyone else. You know that childhood puppy love—whatever you can call it—all I know is it was love for me. She was so mature in her thinking, and she had a great sense of humor, but I was such an ignorant boy. We went through a lot together! She stood by me, but as years went by, we all made our choices, and life took us in different directions. Right now, she is happily married. She will always be a special friend. I moved on, and God has preserved someone special for me, and she will be revealed as I move forward in my life's journey probably in my next book.

Somebody Loves You

It came to my consciousness that although I was rejected, it had less to do with me and more a lot to do with those rejecting me. You see, wisdom is a principal thing, but in all you're getting, get understanding. Choose wisdom as a child. There are things your parents might never reveal to you until you are of age, and it wouldn't be of much importance for them to tell you than to keep their marriage, so we children sometimes end up victims unless you have responsible parents.

People do have a lot of issues going on. Don't be so surprised if people begin to put others down to gain supremacy. They will feel more superior the more they put you down because they think they are better than you. Don't mind about such; it's their insecurity and not about your worth. Whoever pushes you away just can't handle who you are. Probably you are much more than what they can handle, and that's their problem, not yours.

Remember, Jesus knows how you feel. The word of God says in Isaiah 53:3, "But Jesus knew he was loved by his father." Jesus was despised and rejected by men. No matter what you have been through or what people said about you, you are not rejected by God. You are His chosen one. Find your security in God and not in other people's opinions about you. Play dumb to those who are blind to you.

Although not everybody could understand me, I met this friend in the neighborhood who used to bully me a lot, but he liked me because I was an innocent child. He took me under his roof, and he

took care of me for some time. Now this was in the same neighborhood I grew up in, and I believe my father knew I was around the
neighborhood but; for one year, he never even bothered to find out
where his sixteen-year-old son was! Tell me he cared. All my friends
lived to ask themselves why he never cared where I was. Thank God
for friends, sometimes they never understand you, but if they enjoy
your company, they can tolerate you for some time until curiosity
kicks in.

At some point, this friend of mine had to travel, and I had to
find a life. He traveled to the United Kingdom (London), where he
passed away in an accident but left a brilliant son, Marvin, with a
good upbringing, and he will always be a son to me.

Before he died, he had introduced me to a nightclub. So I
remember I had got a new home. I would walk for three kilometers
every day to go to a nightclub, not that I wanted it, but I never had a
penny to transport me there. And it was the only place I was accepted
without being questioned about my family because I was so young to
be out at such a tender age.

I remember I would get to the club when they had just opened,
like at 8:30 p.m., and then sit around and dance from outside till
about 1:00 a.m. And I would beg the bouncers to let me in for at
least a few hours so I could warm up. Sometimes I would stay outside
the club till morning, and I would walk again for three kilometers
back to my father's porch. I remember sleepwalking for like thirty
minutes to my hideout, and I always wonder how God kept me safe
through all these things. Interestingly, within me, there was no fear
that anything wrong could ever happen to me. I know this because
through it all, I had the courage to endure what I was going through,
and surely, God was my refuge. And I believe He had put angels in
charge over my life. That's why nothing touched me, nor did any
insect bite me.

I always had to make sure nobody ever caught me sleeping in
that bush. I remember in all these situations not having a place to
sleep, food to eat, or clothes to put on. I always asked God to preserve my life and to protect me. I'm always amazed by the never-end-
ing love of God for me, and I kept wondering why the God I had

never seen or known God was so mindful of me and gave me that inner conviction of some type of love and feeling of protection.

I am always reminded of this memory when I went hungry for three days and was almost dying, and I had to go plead to a man who used to own a restaurant and beg him to get me something to eat for about two hundred shillings (twenty-five cents). He looked at me and said he knew my family and wondered what was going on with my life, given that I came from a good family. He asked why I was begging for food to eat in the restaurant instead of going to eat at home. I simply said to him, "I can't." He had a heart of a father, and I believe he was a good man. He gave me a plate of food and a cup of tea. He urged me to go home, but he had no idea what I was going through.

This went on for over two years of being a vagabond, and for sure, it robbed me of my childhood memories. This actually forced me to practice social distancing since I sometimes felt I didn't fit in some societies, but I would force my way in the crowd. On the other hand, surprisingly, I actually had family members who were well-off; and to my knowledge, some were not aware of my situation, for whoever came across me would avoid me and didn't want to associate with me. And the revelation of why that was so came to me when I was of age (dirty little family secrets).

I missed school for over seven years. People I was with in high school joined college, while I was struggling to find a home. I felt so sad having missed school all those years, but since communication wasn't easy those days, in that period, I lost contact with all my childhood and school friends. Gone are the days.

In 1998, as I was walking around in the neighborhood as my routine of loitering was, I came across a cousin-sister of mine named Amelia, who is now living in England. Not knowing what to do with me, I believe she knew who could help me, so she asked me to go to church with her. At first, I hesitated because I wasn't looking okay and not fresh, having not taken a shower for days, but she convinced me and I accepted.

Now this was my first time to get to a gathering with many people. I believe it was a time of praise and worship when we walked in, for people were singing and dancing while lifting their hands. At first, I was like in trouble. These people were crazy, but it was a different crazy because as people were singing and shouting, it seemed interesting; so I felt at home because nobody was concentrating on me, but rather just on the music, singing, dancing, and shouting. I didn't feel any judgment upon me or see people looking at me in a funny way. Everybody seemed preoccupied and soaked in the music, so my burden was lifted.

It got to a point where the music stopped and the preacher came onstage and preached for like thirty minutes. Then he asked for those who were visiting for the very first time. Now, I began shaking. In my mind I was like Solomon! I was not visiting for the first time, but rather, I just got convinced and dragged to come in here. So I waited to get up only when he asked who was dragged. But suddenly, I had the conviction to stand up. When I did, Amelia asked me to go to the front as the pastor had requested. And when I took the first step to stand up, I saw people clapping, chanting, shouting, shaking my hand. Wow, it was a glorious day. I felt special for the first time in my life that I was so happy to even remember what I was wearing or how I looked. That didn't matter to me anymore. For the first time in my life, people seemed to like me so much. Walking fifteen meters to the front felt like one hundred meters. All I did was face the front and just walk. It was the longest journey I ever walked, but I'm glad I did.

Getting to the front, I was asked if I wanted to give my life to Jesus, and I had no idea what he was talking about, although I had a good feeling about it. So I said, "Yes," and the house went crazy happy. And just like when people get excited when a man proposes to his future wife, I believe that was my proposal. And I believe the whole heaven shook in gladness and joy when I said yes.

I can imagine all angels saying among themselves, "He said *yes!*" But anyway, people seemed happy for me for making such a decision. Now, before I went to church, I was very hungry, but as I walked in, I forgot about my hunger for the next four hours. And by the time I left, I had made more friends in those four hours than I ever made in my seventeen years. Now this reveals to me that good decisions always have fruits that come as a result. Since then, I'm always conscious of making good decisions.

Have I made just the right decisions since then? Nope. But I always make sure I do my best.

Well, now that was a new beginning on May 20, 1998, when I got saved and gave my life to Jesus. I met new friends who were genuinely interested in me and wanted me to be a part of their lives. These were young people who were in church and were interested to start up a dance group in church. Just to mention a few, Saul Mulindwa, Kigazi Brian, Herbert Sembatya, Jackie Tino, Aguti Joan, and Patricia. I was so eager to join them since I knew I was a good dancer, and I did.

A Second Chance

During the same year, I decided to give home another chance; but when I got there, I found things changed a lot and were not the way they were.

First of all, I found my grandmother had visited but had bedridden for almost two months, per what I was told, and hadn't been to a doctor since that time my dad was not around. My grandmother was ninety-eight years old. She had been neglected in bed for that long, and she had terrible bed sores. I went in, and she smiled like she had seen the light. I put shame aside, picked her up, cleaned her and her bed, washed everything, and freshened her up. Then I made her a cup of tea. She couldn't talk, but I could see that she was so embarrassed for a grandson to do all that. But when all the cleaning and dressing was done, she smiled at me. I told her I loved her. She was so sweet, and I always loved it when she smiled with her wrinkles. I wish she said a word, but pain couldn't let her open her mouth.

After I had stayed for a day at home, my dad got back, and I was worried, thinking this time he was going to kill me. But he heard that I had done a great job with Grandma. His temper cooled, but he never thanked me for what I had done, neither did he ask me where I had been all those years. And that was all I needed to hear, at least to feel that he cared. I was fragile that time, and I needed somebody to tell me that they actually cared. But anyway, he didn't and has never, but I moved on.

The next day, Grandma was in so much pain, so I asked my father whether I could take her to the hospital, and he said yes.

I organized transportation and took her to the hospital. On reaching there, the doctors concluded that she was to be admitted immediately, and I said yes on her behalf since she couldn't talk because of the pain she was going through. I went back home and left her admitted and told my father that she was admitted. He was angry that I had let her be admitted, but I had done the right thing. He had no choice given the fact that something had to be done, and besides, he had phobia about sick people.

Granny spent three months in the hospital, and I was her attendant and caregiver for all those three months. I bathed her, washing and feeding her through tubes. And the only food she could have were juice, porridge, and soup. I had to use a syringe to pump the food into the tube. It wasn't easy, but what else could a grandson do with his granny but to love her? She was helpless and never said a word in those three months. It felt like I was nursing a baby.

I would do all my chores for her comfort; then afterward, I would go to church in the afternoon. I would then get back to the hospital after church and sing to her a few songs I had learned from church each day, and all she could do was smile. She had a beautiful smile.

My father never came to the hospital to see her in those three months, and I was so mad at him because I could never figure out why, till later, when I realized that he has this phobia about sick people and he just couldn't stand hospitals. Still I couldn't buy that excuse, for this was his mother. However, he is a man who I have never heard complain of any sickness in all the years I've known him.

My granny is a lady who had raised many people who held big positions in the government, but only few knew or saw her during her last days or visited her.

After three months, she had fought her battle but lost, and she passed away while I was at church as a routine I had every evening when she had slept off.

Getting back, I found an empty bed. I knew she had rested and gone to meet her maker. RIP, Granny Mariam Kebikuru.

After her burial, I went back home, but I wasn't happy with the way the whole issue was handled! I know I had taken care of my granny with love, and I was surprised my existence during her suffering wasn't talked about by anybody. And that hurt since I was the only person who stepped in to help of all the people who could have done their part. Despite my disappointment, I can't fail to mention my uncle Charles Karabarinde with pride (who by the way is one of the longest-serving pilots in Uganda with an outstanding legacy). He always appreciated me for what I did for his auntie. I will always remember him for that, for at least one person got to appreciate me. Not that I did it for anybody, but out of love, but it's human to appreciate one another.

He Is Human like You

Forgiveness.

No disrespect, but at some point, I regarded my father's actions as inhumane—the neglect, rejection, and abuse—but every time I looked in the mirror, it was him reflecting in the mirror, for there seemed to be unfinished business that I had to face my fears. The fact is, he wasn't there for me, and he neglected us. I have never heard my father say he loves me or my brother because he has never said it. You see, we all want to be loved, and every child deserves love from their parents regardless.

At some point, I called my father and told him I loved him, and he went silent. Parents, please swallow your pride and holler back. I do not want to judge him though; maybe somewhere, somehow, he did love me. I choose to look at it like that, although I have always longed to hear him say that to me someday. However, I will choose to believe him whenever he chooses to say it.

There were too many hurtful memories of my childhood, but I had a life to live. My pastor Robert Kayanja always sang a song:

> Your latter will be greater than the past,
> You will be blessed more than you could ask,
> In spite all that has been done,
> The best is yet to come, and your latter will
> be greater,
> Your latter will be greater than the past
> All things are possible, possible, possible,
> And your latter will be greater than the past.

35

I started to realize that my future is not dictated by my past, and the only way to move forward is to learn how to forgive. Forgiveness enables you to free yourself.

Forgiveness is a decision, not a feeling. I had to forgive my father. And before I did, it felt like I had a debt I hadn't paid. But now I am free! You too can free yourself by beginning to forgive those who hurt you in the past. The fact is you don't have to forgive them, but you have to because it is for your own freedom! Freedom cannot be bought! You have to fight for it. But in this case, you just have to look back and do the math. Holding on to something against somebody adds no value to you and rather brings you grief and hate, which could result in a lot of serious issues in your life, including sickness.

People whom you have grudges against never experience what you experience. They never feel the pain you do. They are free from what you are feeling, and they don't even care what you are going through. I would rather choose forgiveness because it frees your entire being and brings peace. It's like a dawning of a brand-new day, and I live as a free man. I have chosen forgiveness, and it has affected my life in a positive way. It has helped me to have a deeper understanding of how I should deal with people and has given me a sense of patience I have never had before, and I am a joyful person. And that deeper, unexplainable joy has driven a lot of kindness toward people. It has taken away selfishness, and now before I complain about what's not happening to me, I look around and appreciate that which I have been able to attain and acquire in this beautiful life. My friend Centa Terry always says, "Life is good." Not that all is well, but believing all shall be well, for the Lord is good, and His mercy endures forever. A stress-free life!

You First

I want you to pause a bit and think about the people with whom you have issues and take a step of faith. Maybe start by making a phone call. Mend that relationship with somebody. Let there be a fresh start. Your decision is a declaration of a new day of freedom. You will realize that you saved the day. I understand it's not an easy decision, but it's worth it, and it will unleash a great deal in your life and those you have forgiven. The things that hold your breakthrough are sometimes tied on a thread; and because of fear, anger, and so on, we look at that thread as a chain, but there's power in the blood of Jesus that can break every chain. And it's hidden in the truth, in the knowledge of his word, for the truth you know shall set you free.

When somebody hurts you, your first thoughts would be that they don't deserve forgiveness. We long to see how they can pay back for all that they have done to us. Well, for sure they don't, and the fact is neither do we.

We didn't deserve Jesus's sacrifice of dying on the cross for us, but he did it anyway, and he gave us his forgiveness because he loved us so much. In Mathew 18:21–35, a parable is told of a master who forgave his servant a huge debt, but that same servant refused to forgive a smaller debt that his fellow servant owed him and put him in jail. When the master heard this, he then refused to forgive him of his huge debt.

You need to realize that how much you forgive others is the same amount of grace and forgiveness you will receive.

You need to experience the freedom of forgiveness when you forgive those who did you wrong. Maybe you could start by making a phone call to that person, or writing them an e-mail—whatever you do, free yourself. Imagine flashing a clogged-up sink. There's a new world hidden in forgiveness, but it's on the other side. It's all hidden in you.

If you think you can hurt those who hurt you by being bitter and resentful toward them, you are only hurting yourself. I could talk about so many benefits of forgiveness, but I want you to take a step and have an experience of your own and tell your testimony someday to somebody else. Don't forget to share your experience after you have been set free.

Don't be resentful. It will only bring sadness, and it will affect every part of your personality. It will stain your character, which will eventually have effect on your destiny.

But remember, you have a choice. I choose to honor my father not because he deserves it but because he is my father, the person responsible for my being. To you it might be a mother, friend, boss, friend—you name it. Treat them well likewise. Choose to honor your parents no matter what has gone on all your life. That's the only position they hold that nobody can replace. They are irreplaceable.

Later that year, I resumed going to church. Then after I got involved in ministry, and I felt a new life had begun for me. As if that wasn't enough, one day I met somebody who got concerned about my well-being, and for sure, God's favor started following me. She got concerned about my education and where I stayed. Generally, she wanted to be involved in my life.

My mother was a poor woman who also couldn't do much for me, so God sent me a mother who treated me like her own. I told her my story, and she was so moved that she asked me so many questions. She asked me what I wanted to do, and I told her I wanted to go back to school. So she asked me to look for a school that I wanted, and I thought it was a joke. Well, that week I looked for a school and I got it, and in the next few days, she gave me all the money I needed to start. I cried. I didn't know how to thank her. As if that wasn't enough, she said it was okay for me to stay at her house with her children. I said, "Thank you, Jesus." It was a prayer answered because I needed a home, and God gave me one.

And for some time, I have been a son and a friend of their family to this day—much love to Priscilla, Peter, Benji, John, Judith, Samuel, Sandra, Sharon and Sherry, and Sharon and Sylvia. Thank you for being my friends and family.

Mommy Alex Namaga, you will always be a part of my life and my family. Thank you for your support even when it was hard for you. You loved me unconditionally and took care of me. May God bless you and your family abundantly. Living with Mommy Alex, I made a lot of mistakes, but she was always there for me. I managed to sit for my ordinary level exams.

I had to face the responsibility of being a young father, and even then, Mommy Alex still showed love to my daughter that time when life was so challenging.

Before I had Mercy, I had a son, Kevin, who was then two years old. In me was a longing to have a family. I didn't know where life would take me, and I needed guidance in my life, which was full of mistakes like we all do. But I took my responsibility.

That season was also too challenging, but life had to move on. I also thank my brother Cliff, who was always there for me when I most needed him, I love you, brother. I can't forget my mom who would do anything she could. She was such a great cook, the best in town!

Be Grateful

In life, we meet a lot of people, friends, loved ones, enemies, pass-ersby, visitors, haters, and all sorts of people. After some time, you ask or wonder what they refer to you as! And you wonder what they think of you! Well.

Anyway, there are people who just can't get off your heart, people who were there for you when you most needed them. To me, I don't have many. When I needed a place to lay my head, when I needed water to drink or something to eat, they gave all that to me. They were friends and parents to me; they loved me secretly but publicly blessed me. I am so grateful for the man of God Pastor Robert Kayanja. You will always be remembered and talked about wherever I go. You were so kind to me and gave me a chance to better myself. You believed in me! I remember I needed a place to stay, and the world had turned upside down on me. I was so young; I was only seventeen, and you gave me hope. From that bridge, I started seeing my future, and for sure, it is greater. Thank you!

When life was pushing me in a corner with child responsibilities, I ended up occupying myself with voluntary work at church (Miracle Center Cathedral). I was involved in the music department, tried some singing. I also volunteered in the children's ministry for about nine years. Life was changing. I met many friends who became family. Church became a place I called home away from home, and I was always encouraged by the men of God. It was always a pleasure to hear Pastor Robert Kayanja preach.

During my time at the Miracle Center, there were many people around me, but Pr. Martin stood out. He had this similarity to Pr. Robert, and he was so patient with people. He loved you the way you came in, praying that God would do a great work on you.

After ten years of voluntary work around church, I met a friend through whom I managed to get my first job working with children under Rev. Tomi Mills for two years. It was such an amazing experience in my life. She was a great woman and a good friend. Although she was a very stubborn American redhead, she will always be a friend. After the two years, I had to move on with my life. I traveled to the United States and connected with Kimberly, and I don't know how, but I lost focus and lost my job. I took my job for granted; I didn't play my cards right.

Nonetheless, I started up a project of my own, which only lasted five months because I still made some mistakes. I worked with Kimberly Mcghee, who got so interested in the project, so we started an organization called Peaceful Hearts, Uganda. It was so unfortunate we couldn't work together, though I always wished it worked out. She was an amazing person with wonderful children, McKenna, Jenner, Steven, and Keagan. After that, life became a bit challenging. I lost my first job, my project got messed up, and I took the blame for all my losses!

During my time with Tomi, I met many special people who have been a blessing to me. I met Claudia Black from Tirol, Austria. She was and will always be a special friend to me and my family. She always blessed my heart. She encouraged my family however stubborn she was. We shared a lot together. She actually introduced me to white chocolate and always made sure she sent me a piece or two! She has always been close and a blessing to me.

In the same period, I met a great family—Centa Terry, Joey, Josh, Mandy, Terry, Jeffery, and James—who live in Las Vegas, Nevada. I had a great time with them in Nevada. I felt at home and much loved. They are my family too.

I also met another family from Minnesota while I was in the USA. I visited them in their beautiful country home. When I met the children, I didn't know much about them besides the love they extended toward me after I had connected with their mother Tracy whom I call Mom. When Tracy cooked, I felt so much at home. I miss the food there. Moms always have something cooking, and you never feel hungry until they are in the kitchen. Dave was like a dad to me.

While staying at their house, I can't forget their youngest son, Jacob (Jake), who gave up his bed for me for two weeks for a couch! He gave up his comfort for me! Jake, I respect you, brother, and love you lots. It's so challenging how some kids do things. I have never surrendered my bed. You all know it's hard to let go of your bed for two weeks! A child with such a big heart—I strongly believe he will be a great guy when he grows up.

Work Gives You Status

Now if you have worked before or are working now, but taking work for granted, remember the friends you have made simply because you choose to work where you are working, people you never knew before.

I happened to like some restaurants in town. I was always on the lookout for a new restaurant, but I always found myself meeting up friends at this particular restaurant.

In my home city, Kampala, there was a famous restaurant named Nandos. Nandos was a place I always went to hang out with friends in the evenings and share a cup of tea—good moments and memories. I still think they have the best chicken. I happened to be a friend of one of the waiters, who always offered his services with a smile. He was not your ordinary waiter; he was very talkative, but that was okay. He was a cool, studied guy with very good English! The waiting job is a much-despised job in Kampala; many times, waitstaff are treated like trash. The irony of this though, in my observation, is that people who treat waitstaff like trash are the very people who cannot afford even a cup of tea. These individuals would shamelessly order one teapot to go around the entire party, just with extra tea bags! As if that was not an embarrassment enough, they would ask the waitstaff for their digits.

I never knew how that worked! Funny. Anyway, this friend of mine who was a waiter shocked me one day when we had a little chat. He told me he was getting married soon, and I just could not believe it! So to prove to me that he was serious, he invited me to the wedding, which I wasn't able to attend, but I apologized for that. But it was a wonderful wedding. His wife was beautiful. You wouldn't think she would say I do to him, but she did. A waiter getting married? Yes, he did from his little earnings. He was able to take care of his wedding bills. He is now a father of a very handsome boy. He gained the status of being an honorable man and a father because he understood the importance of his job and work. True story. Looking back at his life, he made the right choices. He is moving on and happily married with children.

Work continued.

Work is a gift from God. Work will always bring you honor. You are designed to meet the needs of your life through work. When you refuse to work, you delay yourself. The only way you can prove that you can do something is by accepting to do it first.

Work will always give you a better life, whereby you will be able to meet your financial needs and responsibilities. I remember a period in my life when I was renting a two-bedroom house, and I had not been working for some time. The landlady would knock so hard on my bedroom window very early in the morning, demanding rent. Inasmuch as I hated that, if I had been working, I would have been able to pay up my rent to avoid all that. When you work, you will never go hungry! I came to realize that when you do not work, you become a burden to others; but when you go to work, you can avoid that too! Go get a job and meet those needs! It's never too late; otherwise, you will complain all your life.

Work Brings Esteem

Come to think of it: before you land a job, most times you feel like you do not belong to some circles of friends; but when you start working, there is an enhancement in your esteem. In life, if you ever feel worthless, just find work to do and keep yourself busy. You will see the results of how you feel about yourself. You are feeling bad about yourself, being broke and isolated because you are lazy. Go find a job. Whenever you take the opportunity to focus on the results of your labor instead of your lack in life, thinking that no one cares or loves you, and feeling incapable, you will start to feel good about yourself, and you will appreciate yourself more.

Tips and Advice

Looking back but you have a happy life. If a guy doesn't want to communicate, it's a sign that he doesn't want to commit himself to that relationship, or he is scared to commit. Although sometimes that is not the case; guys don't say much especially when they have financial issues. Don't just think he is cheating, understand your partner!

Are you an addict? Sober up.

Look here. You have to sober up now and give me your ear.

Growing up as a young man, I have come across many people, and I have come to realize one thing: "you are what you make of yourself." People will always call you what you have named yourself. If you spend more time on music or associating yourself with musicians, people will start calling you a musician. Don't be fooled though! Dancing to other people's music doesn't necessarily make you a musician any more than sitting in a garage would make you a car. If you happen to be going around terrorizing your neighborhood, people in your society will call you a thug. And when you are the kind of guy who messes up with every girl in your neighborhood, you will be called a womanizer.

Many times, we get judged for the things we have done but blame people for judging us. However, if you come to think of it, you got yourself in that exact spot where you are. You might have been good or bad; still, you are what you have made of yourself. And if you had chosen to do otherwise, you would have been called exactly what you wish people would call you. Have you ever asked yourself these questions? "Who am I?" "What do people call me?"

Whatever answer comes out of your head is exactly what your position is majority of the time.

Tell you what, take some time and look back on where you have come from! Stop making excuses or blaming other people for your faults. You cannot change your past. What happened did happen, and it's done. It's a new day. You can change how you think by moving forward, and that begins with a positive thinking. Stop thinking about what you think other people are thinking of you. People actually don't care much most of the time. But God does. People will only begin to care when you take the first step to becoming a better person. First and foremost, stop beating yourself up. Before, people might have looked at you and saw a mess; but when you get up and fight to make yourself a better person, you will be surprised that people will get the message and begin to look at you differently. Your actions are the glasses through which people look to judge your progress.

I have a brother who was raised by great parents. He was taken to the best schools in the country in his time, and he was a very smart child while growing up with such a warm heart toward others, and he is still an interesting fellow today. Oscar is his name.

Oscar had a lot of friends, all of whom were from outstanding families with successful backgrounds since he too was from a prominent family. Being in school as a child, Oscar seemed to be very interesting and adventurous, and so were his buddies. At some point, Oscar and his friends started using drugs and becoming wasted, which wasn't a good thing for him being in school. He started missing school, and the worst thing happened. Oscar missed his final exams that would have taken him to university because he was high. It was so absurd that along the way he lost both his parents who would have guided him in the right path, which was really sad and hard for him to take as a child. However, that geared him more toward drugs. Oscar was a promising child to all his family. Many looked up to him thinking he would be one of those great people in the country because of his outstanding grades in school, but his friends introduced him to drugs and messed him up. Everybody lost trust in him, and nobody wanted to be associated with him. Most of his friends and some family members deserted him when they realized that he had become an addict, apart from his great friend Allan, who remained loyal to him and gave him a shoulder to lean on when he could. Such friends aren't many. Oscar never wanted, nor had ever desired, to be in such a position, but he got himself there. He could never blame it on anybody but himself.

But thank God for family members who were there to support him and love him when it was hard for the rest, when everybody gave up on him, some people did not; they had hopes in him. Today, Oscar, who was an addict for over two years, is becoming a better person each day that goes by. His brother Eric, who is my cousin and a good friend, managed to get Oscar his first job in thirty years, and now he is able to earn a living and take care of a few personal needs. Another brother named Emma, who also could never sleep because his brother wasn't doing well, was so supportive; and he did all he could to make sure Oscar never lacked a thing.

I remember a time when Emma asked me to look for any ways possible to see to it that Oscar got help irrespective of the cost, and that's what I call true brotherhood. Oscar might have never known what all these people did, but someday he will read it in my book. And he will know that even when he was so high, somebody still cared and loved him so dearly each day. Everybody was hurting with him because they believed in him.

Oscar is a father of three as I speak, and he is able to look and see his children with a sober mind. Because Oscar made a decision and chose to move forward to experience a better life, now his children are also proud to call him dad. He gave himself a second chance for them to have the only chance to have their father back. Now everybody recognizes him as the father of his children. Each day I see him getting better and blessed.

Oscar must have looked back and realized that he was the last chance to make himself a better man, so he made the right decision to move forward. I don't think it was easy for him, but day by day, it's getting better. He looks at life from a different angle with a sober mind. Everybody has a story about his past. "What is your story?" "What is your decision?" You might not have been like Oscar, but you too have your own story to tell. Make that decision to be a better person. Look at Oscar. He changed and determined what people are going to call him. I am proud of you, Oscar. And I believe your mom and dad would have said those exact words if they had seen you make such great decisions to get back on track.

I believe you don't appreciate yourself right now for having gotten yourself into some mess, but no one is perfect. We have all made wrong turns at some point in life. There are things we did that society had no choice but to abandon and reject us. You might have been on drugs. Maybe you have been abused by family or a friend. Well, a time comes when you have to put everything behind you. I know it really hurts, but remember where you have come from. Look at your current situation; then reflect on whom you have become and who you want to be. What do you want your future to look like? Well, you can blame every stage on anybody, but at the end of it all, it is still about you. Whatever decision you make today will affect your future in a positive or negative way, but you determine that.

There is a chance to get your life back on track and move forward, for the future holds a better life. You can choose to have a sober future by making that decision to move forward. You are a great person with lots of gifts and talents. Somebody out there is just waiting to see you make that smart choice, and then they will look you up. Trust me, there is a lot out there still just for you, if only you look back and make that decision in your heart to quit drugs, drinking—name it all.

Many people are proud of you, but you won't believe they even care unless you isolate yourself from those peers who keep dragging you back to your old habits. It is your responsibility to show them that you are not the same person you used to be, that you are taking a step to break away from that addiction that is ruining your life slowly by slowly.

You might have lots of great dreams, but they can only happen in the sober world. Don't trust flying with wings when you are high; you will crush. You might even have dropped out of school when you started that habit, but you can still catch up with school. It's not too late. You can start from where you left off.

May be your family abandoned you when you started on those drugs. Well, I believe they are waiting for you at home. Get back home and let them see that you are sober. They will tell you one thing: welcome back home.

You don't want to miss those great meals at home, do you? Make that decision today. You can still fit in. Everybody is saying you can do it, but they are waiting to celebrate with you only if you say, "I can do this!" And I believe you can, so go on and do it! Yes, you can do it! Do it today, now! Give up that habit. Give up those drugs. Drop that weapon and move on. You will never regret making this decision. Drop it and don't look back. Your life will never be the same again. And it's okay to cry and forgive yourself for those whom you have hurt just because of the bad decisions you made in the past. They are ready to forgive you after you make that decision. May you be led by the grace of God as you receive your redemption.

If you dared yourself into an addiction, you can still dare to dream to get back on track and do great things for yourself and your family.

- ➢ Dare to go back and finish university.
- ➢ Dare to get back your family's trust.
- ➢ Dare to get that job that you lost or a better one.
- ➢ Dare to make that relationship work again and take it to the next level. If you got high while dating, start afresh and think about proposing. Don't waste any more time.
- ➢ Dare to get back to church and watch how God's love embraces you.

You need to desire the best of you, though it might not be easy. Just dare!

Find a good friend and share with them your life, and accept them to help you. However, you have to be daring to step up aggressively, and watch out who influences you this time around. Remember, whomever you spend most of your time with will determine your next image in the community. Something might be challenging in the process, but you got to take the challenges that come along the way. You will start hearing sweet rumors about your progress. If you press on, great things await you, dear friend. You will be proud of whom you will become!

Slowly but surely, you will discover who you really are, from nobody to somebody!

Real life is when you live life the way you should while sober, doing things the right way. Life is good, and you know that. Be determined to enjoy it and inspire others to be better people. It doesn't end with you. Somebody helped you to help another. Pass on the love. It is a possibility that you might go back to some of the friends you got high with and try to get some back to reality. I believe you will be a very good example to them. Your progress determines their fate. Help somebody out there.

There's a great leader in you. Focus and you will see that all will come to manifest. You have to come face-to-face with yourself with questions and answers. Enjoy life again as it unfolds a new chapter or leaflet each day. When all is said and done, you will look back and appreciate the experiences and what they have formed in you to make you this new person.

Discipline

Most times in life, we intend to ignore what's so important, thinking of it as just being normal, yet most times what we ignore are the keys to great success.

I wish I knew what discipline meant while growing up. Many times, we wish to get things out of excitement and go through emotional displays, but we are not willing to do what is necessary to get the results we want.

Today, most people are so successful because they knew the secret of discipline. You might know what discipline is and yet not disciplined.

What is discipline?

Discipline is a training that corrects, molds, or perfects mental faculties or moral character. It is the reason why some people are better than others. Without discipline, you can't enjoy a winning life. You ought to be disciplined in all corners of your life if you want to achieve your goals. Discipline molds your character.

I have come to realize that when you discipline yourself in whichever way, things will always work out for you. Discipline sets things in motion. Let's look at it in our normal lives.

If you discipline yourself to jog every evening—how you spend your money, how you eat—you will realize that every day you take that step, you will be moving forward. Choose to take a discipline step today, and see how life sets all your endeavors in motion.

Persistence

Life! Generally, life isn't just an easy path. We grow up being taken care of by our parents, if you give them the chance to be there for you, or somewhere, somehow, somebody helped you grow up.

It is an individual endeavor to work hard, to fight and see that you make it in life.

Life isn't all about guitars. It's all about people who fail and then get back up and give it another try.

Don't ever think that you are now done, calling yourself a failure. The fact is you only fail when you don't intend to try again.

The fact is, the next time you give yourself another chance, your success awaits you!

Remember, quitters never win and winners never quit. If someone else made it in life, if they bought a car, built a house, made it to university, you too can achieve that. Never say never. Always build positive walls around your brain, and be determined to win in life no matter what.

Success is yours. Grab ahold of it and do not let doubt steal it from you. The fact is that nobody can take it from you because it's already what you're made of.

There's somebody in you that the world is waiting for; loosen him or her up. That great potential lies on the inside of you and needs to be exposed. Expose your ability.

You Talk Too Much

Always watch your mouth! It's good to know when to talk and when not to.

Personally, I sometimes talk too much, and after some points, I realize, oops, I said something. Well, not the bad words but saying things that shouldn't have been said to certain people. Learn to keep secrets.

Don't discuss people, discuss issues. And at the end of the day, problems will be solved.

Be slow to speak. Be the last to speak. Listen more before you contribute to a conversation. Remember, too many words might make you lose friends. Always speak the truth in love, because sometimes speaking the hard truth out of love can be considered arrogance.

Sometimes, you don't have to speak unless you are asked to.

The reason why some people are out of work is that at some point they had a job but didn't obey the rules of that job.

Solomon's Words of Wisdom

An invincible determination can nearly accomplish anything you put your mind to, whatsoever you choose to do in life.

Be determined to get good results out of it. Squeeze the juice out of every situation rather than complaining all the time.

Let nothing get you to a point of quitting. You rather fail but don't fail to try. Don't be a quitter. Don't be a person of compromise.

Refuse to be a laughing stock. Someday you will come out a winner and victorious.

Listen to your heart more than you listen to anybody. Your inner being always has the right answers to most of life's questions. Listen to that still small voice in you that tells you to do what is right. He will guide you always because you are not a being of your own making, but God's, specially created in His image. Always seek knowledge of what you are truly made of.

Attitude

I have come to realize that the number one key to acquiring and failing to acquire knowledge or success is attitude. Your attitude will determine your altitude.

Your attitude will determine how quick you learn. Take, for example, applying for a new job, and when you get that job you have been waiting for, your boss gives you a junior to take you through some procedures to ease your work. Well, he could be your junior, but he might have more experience at that job than you do. Your attitude toward his efforts will determine his output of the information he is supposed to share.

Attitude will break you or make you.

Attitude will earn you success.

The question is "what is your attitude toward the things and people you associate with or toward life?"

But what is interesting is that you can determine all that by controlling your attitude and not letting your attitude control you.

Kindness

I heard a voice while walking along the street. "Help, please… Help!" It seemed like a little child's voice. I pretended not to have heard it. A little hand won't cost you anything! Still, the voice continued. I remained on my phone, attending to my calls.

The next day, I was passing on the same street and heard a kid who always begged there died of hunger. I still hear that voice saying, *A little hand won't cost you anything.*

Availability

You are only the best when you are in your position. If you don't guard it, there is always a replacement. Avoid being your own disappointment. Be focused and stick to your plans. And most importantly, be available even when there is no work. Opportunity is always looking for a valid address. Your presence qualifies you, and hard work is always celebrated, although it's good to work smart.

When you discover who you are, that's one of the greatest achievements in your life because at least you know where to start now that you have started, which is A in the alphabet, the beginning. B to Z are waiting. They are aware of you, and without you, they can't be. Don't keep them waiting for long. Dig your foundation before the builders join you! Be the designer of your life! And make it!

Faith

Faith isn't a jump in the dark, it's a walk in the light. With faith, don't just guess. You know and believe it works out for the good reasons! I have come to realize that anything you carry from your thoughts to your actions is within your power to achieve or accomplish!

Gates are not doors; they are just passwords that can get you to the door! Similarly, humility can earn you favor!

In relationships, our partners are always giving us at least 80 percent of what we expect of them. We tend to think a lot is missing that we start looking elsewhere, but many times we find what we have been looking for, not knowing that 20 percent was missing in your first relationship. Always work on your relationship. It's a garden; water it every day.

Stick to your spouse. You can only feel closer to each other when you fail, forgive, persevere, and press on together.

Friends

We all love friends, and we love to be friends with somebody. The question is, are you a true friend? I have come to realize that people who call themselves your friends are most oftentimes not your friends. In most cases, these are people who want you simply because of what they can get from you. You are just a shelter until you run out of what they need from you. They then become the press. They seem to know and say everything about you! The minute it's broken down, they look for another shelter.

I love my daughter because I know she is my friend. No matter what I look like, she will always call me dad! Well, with my son, we are blood friends! He has no choice; he is all me!

Not everyone who calls you friend is a true friend. They scratch your back. Most friends are hypocrites. I have friends who hurt me and pretend to be my friends.

As a young person, a young lady or a young gentleman, you need to know how to categorize your friends. There are friends who bring the best out of you, and the best of you comes out in different ways.

There are also friends who bring the worst out of you. They want to see you drunk. They want you to join them and miss school. They will encourage you to sleep with that man to get that job. At some point, they might tell you, or ask you, why you are abstaining! Now for such friends, you need to know who they are and draw the line. Not good influence!

Then you find the kind of friends who always care about you, asking you where you have been till late at night and who that guy is that you are seeing, ascertaining if you really know him, questioning why you didn't you go to lectures, wondering if you are okay, and asking if there is anything you need! Many times, we do not like such friends who prey on our personal lives, but I have come to realize that the biggest percentage of such friends are the ones who care and are genuine that we don't have to push away. Sometimes their voices are a warning. Don't just turn a deaf ear. Stop and give them some time.

You might have more than what they have, but they are important. You can't ignore a sign that warns you of a ditch a head; you will break yourself!

Study your life so that you make the right choice of people you want to surround yourself. You know your friends better than anyone. Study why they are around you and why you are around them, and make wise decisions. After all, it's your life.

Just like your mom taught you while growing up, always take the trash out. You don't keep trash in the house. So why keep that which you really know you don't need in your life? It's never too late to do that. Even at your work, know who your boss is! Draw the line.

Begin today and study your surroundings. You might need to throw some trash out. Looking back on life, some of us didn't have a chance to know all that, but we have learned from our mistakes. Count yourself lucky; someone has to share his life.

Do You Think about Your Parents?

I wish you, being a child in school, at some point stop whatever you are doing and ask yourself, how does Mom or Dad, Aunt, or Granny manage to take care of my school needs, from my very first class to university.

Most times in life, parents never tell you what they go through to get your school fees! But trust me, many parents go through a lot. Some have lived with debts just because you had to go to school. Every parent in their position has sacrificed a lot for you to go to school so that you get to a point where by you can stand on your own, and perhaps take care of your siblings and your future.

This is what bothers me. Sometimes we take all this for granted just because we do not know the sacrifices our parents make. I wish you take some time off and ask your parents how they were able to educate you! And after all is said and done, say thank you. You do not have to wait until you graduate to say thank you. Encourage them whenever you can. Do not just suck everything out of them without depositing any gratitude!

Everybody in life wants to be appreciated, so do parents. Respect them by honoring their effort! Be in school when you have to. Do your part and study. By the time you realize it, all will be done!

Look here! Your parents wish the best of you to come out. Do not disappoint them! I know in this generation kids say they want to have some fun, but listen to me closely! You need to be focused in life.

Fun is good, but if you do not have it at the right time, you dig for your own failure. Do not be influenced by others in doing what is not right!

As for drinking, I know many kids in secondary or high school want to taste beer, but listen up: the minute you taste it, you are wasted, and you set yourself on the journey to destruction. I will share a few stories to drive this home. Follow along.

I once had a friend who was joining university (freshman). She had earlier lost both her parents, a predicament that was not easy for her! I loved her like a sister. She used to fancy good things that she could not afford. So one day, some dude had a crush on her, and they dated for a few weeks and went to nightclubs and bars. Now this guy knew the girl wanted goodies, so once in a while, he provided some. Sadly, one day this guy demanded returns that the girl wasn't ready to let go! Being in the guy's car and drunk, he ended up raping her! Now that was really sad, but thank God we arrested the guy.

But looking back at all this, although the girl's parents were gone, she had guardians. She didn't have to go through an unfortunate situation! That is why I urge you to look out for one another while in school. Avoid drinking while in school.

Before you do something, think about your parents and what they go through to get you to where you are, so make the right choices.

Lessons

Listen to your parents; they are not just being hard on you! They do care about you and love you more than any of your friends.

Refuse to be pushed into programs you didn't plan for, house parties in which you hardly know the host.

Surround yourself with people who have gained your trust. Choose your friends based on character, not on appearance.

Be grateful with the little you have and enjoy it. Call your family more than you call your buddies. The home phone lines will never be busy for you, and actually, they are always waiting for your call.

Ask for Permission

Every time you have to sneak out to do something, there is most likely trouble awaiting you!

Let me share this story with you. I had a friend who was at university. She had this roommate who had just joined campus but what was interesting. This freshman had a boyfriend, and she would sleep out five days a week, missing lectures at the same time. She did this for quite some time. What is so sad is that she never informed her roommate where she was spending most of her time.

One night, as she was coming from a nightclub on a motorbike at 4:00 a.m., she had an accident and was admitted for some time; and the doctor informed her parents that she needed to rest, meaning she had to have a dead year.

Her parents asked her roommate where she was when the ordeal happened, but poor Tickler didn't know what to answer because she had no idea.

Now look here: you don't have to take your parent through such trauma! Save them the heartache, and save yourself by being responsible with your own life. Please don't just sneak out. Inform somebody about where you are going and with whom you are going.

Leave all the contact details of the person whom you are going with and the place where you are going. Be open to your friends and family. It's the only way they can help you with what you don't know! Fun never ends, and it can wait! When you make the right choices and accept advice from the people who care about you, you will one day look back and won't regret a thing. In life, there is a lot to learn from. You don't have to be a victim of circumstances.

Your future is bright. Choose to move on with life well equipped to face life's challenges. Life is good; live it well.

A Good Wife

Allow me to talk about a wife, although I don't have one yet! But I have a mother, and I believe she would have been a good wife to my father if she wasn't abandoned. My mother is a great woman, having given birth to a wonderful me.

I don't know what's wrong with us men sometimes! You choose to marry a great woman, who turns out to be a great mother to your children, submissive, and then end up in divorce just to bring in a strange woman who can't even cook or take care of you! Only to suffer a chronic disease a few years down the road, and the strange woman is praying that you die so she can have a piece of what you worked for with your wife before you threw her out like a bag of trash. Through all this, the mother of your children is on her knees, praying and begging God to preserve and save the father of her children.

As fathers, I believe you go through lots of experiences; but before those experiences lead you to signing those divorce papers, look back and check yourself, and ask yourself a few questions. Is there anything I can do to avoid losing my wife and my family? Is it all about me, or am I being selfish? Is it greed? And the truth is you know all the answers to all those questions, but all you need to do is make the right decision, looking at all parties, in this situation, your family! Choose not to neglect and abandon your family. And as you look back, asking yourself these questions, choose to take a step forward, a step of faith, and position yourself to move forward with a positive attitude toward the restoration of your family, trusting God to be your mediator.

I strongly believe a relationship can be mended if there is good communication, although some people are very unfortunate that their relationships have to end because of some serious reasons best known to them, and both parties choose to end the marriage. This is so sad because at the end of the day, the children are most impacted by the separation. I salute single parents because it's not an easy task raising children alone. But looking back at all those experiences in somebody's life, you've got to move on and live your life. Don't stop living just because you are a single parent. Get a life.

Now I am not insinuating that men are always the perpetrators in all this; women can sometimes also be very stubborn. I happened to know a certain couple who had two beautiful daughters. Now the husband is a very hardworking man who ensures that his family is comfortable, and they lacked nothing, and his family always came first. He did all kinds of jobs to ensure that the family, and mostly his wife never desired a thing and didn't get it, and he did all that because he loved his wife and family.

But watch this! Most times when the husband would get back from work, hungry and tired, all she could say was, "Hey," as she stayed seated in the couch, watching television and not even giving him a hug. I repeat, she would stay watching TV! The husband would come back carrying groceries, and she couldn't even help him out! Follow me closely. He would get all the groceries and put them away, freshen up, and come back to sit with the wife, and she would still be seated, glued to the TV! Now, I witnessed this! He asked for some food, and she pointed him to where the food was without moving an inch! What I know from the way an African woman is raised is that's wrong. Let's not even say African woman; any good woman has to know how to take care of her man.

That was the character of that woman, and she didn't change much. So one day, her husband and I visited a friend. The host's wife gave us a treat, and the way we were treated made us want to stay with no intention of leaving because we were treated like kings at the table. Food was served; that's my point! Unfortunately, we had to leave, but at the end of the day, as a woman, if you don't take care of your man, you could lose him to another woman just because of the little things you choose to ignore, like feeding him. Don't just point to where the food is when he gets home, tired.

Serve your man dinner or lunch or whatever you have to or maybe a glass of juice on a hot day. Your partner should be your good friend. You ought to know them better, and don't lose the sensitivity of who they are. As a woman, you have the power to keep the romance in your relationship burning fresh.

Help one another because you all need a good day however much everyone has had a bad day, but it takes an understanding and good partner to take you through it.

I believe a man can be so loyal when he is treated right. Some men are really good men, but there is something in a woman that can turn him into anything depending on how he is handled. Some end up messed up, and others turn out to be great men, husbands, and fathers. I hope you don't find this information offensive, but I am trying to help somebody.

Don't be disrespectful to your husband just because he hasn't met the standards for a man that you expected him to be. Have respect for him in his humble beginnings. Disrespecting a man can make him turn into a violent person, which could later ruin a good home or relationship, leading to unnecessary divorce. All that can be avoided if you choose to understand your partner.

I am not saying that this works for everybody. Some relationships are so messed up that it's better to step out before you are stepped on.

But it's always good to get some quiet time by yourself as a person of understanding. Look back at patterns of things that have happened to you or in your relationship.

Check yourself before you judge anybody. Find out where you went wrong, what you did wrong, what you haven't done, and what you could do to make things better tomorrow.

Look back and make decisions that will make you be in a better place. We all seek different things in life, but if it's a relationship, I am talking about a marriage relationship. You can work things out and have a better life. Before you move forward with the decisions you make, sit with your partner together and look back. Remind yourselves of the good and bad times you have shared. You may realize that all that was missing was just good communication with one another. The journey gets interesting when you don't forget where you have come from. It's much better to look back and then move forward, joining hands with your partner, than creating a wall between yourselves. Avoid moving forward alone. It might get cold out there, and you will need somebody to hold you.

You are stronger together. Always remember to pray for your loved one as part of your communication, or take it to another level and take the chance to pray together. You realize I have said a lot around food. So after all is said and done, prepare some good food and enjoy one another's company and celebrate life. Life is good.

It's always amazing when you look back and realize you made the right decision. That brings a lot of peace and joy.

I grew up blaming everybody around me, and at some point, I started blaming myself for all my failures, but then I had to learn and seek forgiveness for myself.

Examine

When you choose to move forward after being beaten down by life experiences—be it taking drugs, not being a good parent, being overweight, having broken relationships, breaking promises, being betrayed, being rejected, and so on—try as much as you can not to give negativity an ear! Try to separate yourself from where those vibes are coming so that you can focus on you becoming a better person that you will appreciate.

Be determined and focused with unbeatable consistency. Find a friend and hang out. Go do some outdoor sports. Stay around happy people. Go to a movie. A lot can rejuvenate the good in you when you step out of your usual routine. You are the champion of your own life. Others are just waiting for you to discover the best of you maximized to full ability. Bring out that champion that the world can celebrate.

Growing up as a young man, I have come across a lot of people, and I have come to realize one thing: you are what you have named yourself. If you spend your time in the music industry, people will call you a musician, but dancing to other people's music doesn't make you one.

When you go around terrorizing your neighborhood, people will call you a thug. And if you mess around with every gal in your neighborhood, you will be called a womanizer. And if you have good morals and great character, you will make a good name for yourself.

Many times, we get judged and put the blame on people for judging us, but when we come to think of it, we got ourselves in that exact place where we find ourselves complaining about. Whether good or bad, you are what you have made of yourself. If you had chosen otherwise, you would have been called exactly what you wish people would call you. Ask yourself these questions: *Who am I?* What do people call me? Whatever answer comes to your head is exactly what your position is.

But guess what, look back where you have come from and stop giving excuses. Stop blaming people for your failures. Change the way you think about yourself. Stop blaming yourself too; rather, figure out how to fix your messes. You can't change your past, but you have the power to determine your future. You can't change the past. It's gone. It's a new day.

You can change how you think by choosing to move forward, and it begins with a positive thinking. Stop thinking about what you think other people are thinking about you. People actually don't care much. But God does. People will only begin to care when you choose to take the first steps to becoming a better person. First of all, stop beating yourself up; rather, get up. Before, people looked at you and saw a mess. But when you get up and fight to be a better person, people will get the message and begin to look at you differently.

I happen to have a brother named Oscar, who was raised by great parents. They took him to the best schools in the country. He happened to be a very smart chap growing up with a personality with a great heart. He was a friend magnet, and all his friends were kids from well-to-do families in my city. Oscar was so adventurous that he, at one point, dared to test drugs, which gave a bad sign in his life.

Oscar and his friends started using drugs of all sorts that put him to waste. He kept dropping out of school with all his friends (bad character corrupts good morals). Worse came to worst when Oscar missed his high school final exams that could have taken him to college, all because he was "high." Amid all that, Oscar lost both his parents, and it's really sad to lose a family member. It was a heartbreaking season in his life. That geared Oscar more toward drugs. He was one of those promising people whom the family and the country would look at, but heights messed him up. At some point, most people rejected him because he was a mess, and nobody wanted to associate with him being an addict. Most of his friends deserted him. Some family members couldn't stand him, although some stood with him through it all, however hard it was, by supporting him to transform, praying for him.

Oscar never wanted to be in such a position, but he got himself there. But thank God for his family, who had been there and took care of him. Oscar is now on a full recovery. He has become a better and responsible person after being high for over twenty-three years. His young brother, who is my cousin, got him a job in his meat transportation company, where he manages to make a little living. That's Oscar's first job in over thirty years.

Emma, another brother of ours, was always so supportive when nobody was. He always looked at Oscar as a brother and not as an addict like some others did and was ready to do whatever it took to get him back on his feet. Thank God Oscar finally got back and is now a father of four beautiful children and is able to see his own children with a sober mind.

Because Oscar made a decision to move forward toward a better life, his kids are proud to call him dad, and the rest see him as a father. As a brother who has watched his entire life, I feel so happy and proud of him, and I want to see him get better each day. He is a champion of his life. He conquered his addiction, and I see him getting blessed.

Oscar must have looked back and realized he is the last chance to making himself a better man, so he made the right decision to move forward. You might not have been an addict like Oscar, but you too have your own story. Whatever it is, choose to be a better person. Be like Oscar. He changed the way people called him.

COVID-19 Experiences

On February 2020, while driving in the city, I noticed that we had been hit by the deadliest pandemic of all time, which caused a lockdown in most countries around the world. Being in America, I thought it would be a different story since it's the most powerful country in the whole world, but we were severely hit too, leaving many people dead and businesses affected. The livelihoods of people were stamped because of the fact that no social gatherings were permitted, causing social distancing to be the new norm. No hugs, no handshakes, but rather, his and byes from a few meters away. Millions of people lost their jobs. Never has the world experienced anything like this, with few answers to what could be the solution or cure for COVID-19, as it is called. Among the brilliant brains from all known universities and organizations, none seemed to have an answer. With everything closed, from shopping malls to restaurants and churches, all people were locked in their homes, waiting for who could be the hero with a solution rather trial-and-error vaccines.

Looking back at all this chaos, everything having been closed down, I realized that nature seems to be reproductive, and it seems to me that there is a new beginning about to happen. It seems like we can live without all these things that keep us separate from one another, things that make us feel better than others, things that occupy our minds rather than spending time with our families, things that make us ignore the sole purpose of our lives and focus on luxury—all these things that are not more important than working together as nations

74

walking in love and unity, respecting one another regardless of color, ethnicity, gender, or origin.

When I look back at all that was happening, to me it was a wake-up call. All had gone wrong. It was a call for correction. A call for redirection. A call to heed instruction. We had idolized things, work, money, all material things. We were so busy and forgot about the God, who enables us to do all these things. A call to return to our first love. A call to remember the giver of life. God loves His people so much that He doesn't want anything that makes them forget about Him.

A year before all this happened, in 2019, I was on a live youth Facebook show called "Untrodden." God gave me a word and told me to share about "paying attention." A lot was going on in my personal life that my spiritual ear didn't pay attention. Had I been obedient to that voice, I would have been able to be a blessing to many during this season or to caution some people to prepare. That's exactly what happens. It's hard to be obedient to what you haven't paid attention to.

As I look back, I chose to learn to pay attention to life, but most importantly, to my spiritual life. I've learned that you gotta be sensitive to your inner voice. I've learned that you need to keep your friends and also be a good friend. But also, I've learned that a man needs to get married. I've never seen such lonely times, wishing I had gotten married then. But God makes thing beautiful in His time; otherwise, everybody needs somebody to love and cherish. When you find a good one, don't just like her. Love her and marry her. All I looked at in that season was my closet, and how I wished I shared a closet with somebody special. Life wasn't easy being by myself. These were trying times for everyone. Everybody had their own experiences. Nobody could get used to not knowing when it will end, but eventually, day by day, you realize that situations come and go.

My condolences to those who lost loved ones during the season to a point where some didn't even get a chance to bid farewell to their loved ones. But life goes on. There are many lessons to learn from all this.

When I look back at all this, I realize that love is the greatest gift of all. Love saved us. Thanks to the first responders who did a great job in saving many, not to mention the nurses, doctors, caregivers, police, army, governors, and city mayors. Thanks to grocery stores that risked opening to serve us, like Stop & Shop, Walmart, Ocean State Job Lot, Whole foods, and Market Basket. Thanks to UPS, IRS, Amazon, Senate, Congress, Republicans and Democrats, kind landlords, and last but not least, our president, Trump, for doing his best, as well as all the leaders of nations around the world. We are grateful. Thank you for all the sleepless and tireless nights and days you sacrificed for us. We are forever grateful. The future will be greater than the past. One world.

Solomon's Inspirations

Sometimes we all get to that point of giving up on something, or you are at that breaking point that the only way to know your capacity to take on the next level is to keep pushing on. There's hope on the edge. When you feel you can't go any farther, let go and let God. The fact that you managed to get this far is a sign that He's been with you all the way.

Every mechanism is designed to great a connection for it to function, and so is every man. There are things and people that are purposed and meant to connect with you so that you operate at your best and take what belongs to you. My prayer for you is that may God connect you to the people you are meant to connect with this year for something great, but also disconnect you from those that make you lose the God connection.

One of the greatest storms is when people think you haven't been through anything, yet secretly, you are dealing with a certain issue. You are in a secret storm and believe in God for a breakthrough, but you are wondering if God really even cares about you. Listen, don't take the presence of a storm as indicating the absence of God. Believe that God is with you, and that storm is about to be silenced in the name of Jesus. God is about to wipe your tears away. Weeping may endure for a night, but joy cometh in the morning. A new day is coming your way. Get ready to celebrate your victory.

What are you consistent about? There's something about you that has to mature for people to see the God in you, and that will determine how your life story evolves. That in itself will define you.

Discover one thing about you that is above your moods, and consistently cultivate it. That in itself can take your life to another level. It's a gift.

Begin to see yourself in the future, and change how you think. How far do you see you can go either mentally, financially, or spiritually? What will people need tomorrow in your society? What do you see as in demand three years from now? Do you see yourself meeting demands?

Position yourself in demand tomorrow when you use your mind to plan for others. What you need will automatically be met.

You will only progress in the things you have already started. So if you have nothing started, then don't expect anything. Set your mind to something. Find something to do that when people are looking for a service, your name will be the brand.

Don't be surprised if your purpose is to help somebody get to the next level so that they can open a door that can lead you to your breakthrough. Begin to see value in others, and help them maximize their God-given abilities. You never know what God has in store for you because what you have been looking for in life could be hidden in what you need to give away (2 Corinthians 5:18). God has done all this. He has restored our relationship with Him through Christ and has given us this ministry of restoring relationships.

In this life, you are either experienced at what you do and your services are needed, or you are an "experiment." If you don't deliver in an expected season, your days are numbered by somebody else. The question is, why let somebody number your days?

Here's the gist: if you experiment something with the experience you have attained, that's invested time. Don't do everything. Be a master at something that will make your services relevant tomorrow. What you master today, tomorrow people will look for. And it will have your name attached to it. God is behind all you do.

Sometimes delays are seemingly painful, but the intentional excellence of some processes is defined by delays. Your life is perfected in the experiences that God allows to come your way. When you understand who you are, then you will agree that certain things are bound to happen to your kind who is heading on a certain journey. You are not missing anything. You are fine. What may seem like a delay is just a stage at which your process is.

Simple mistakes today can be an intrusion or slowdown of progress tomorrow, making life so intricate in its simplicity. Try as much as you can to pay close attention to life. Nothing just happens. All that happens around you should be like an alert to remind you of how important today is. Your tomorrow might pretty much be today, if you only look closer. Don't skip. It's a process.

When too much is going on around you, be aware that something is coming ahead. Don't put much focus on what's happening now; it shall pass. Plan for what might come next.

Whatever you say you can handle yourself, God is probably going to get out of it. Vengeance belongs to God. He searches the hearts and knows how to deal with the issues of the heart. Avoid holding funny grudges and planning revenge. Give yourself some rest. Peace is of the Holy Spirit. Let go and let God fight for you. He never loses.

Chill confidently knowing that He's got you. Soon you will sing a song of victory over what has been bothering you. Just keep confessing, "My God never fails."

When you aren't ready for something, time flies so fast. But when you prepare yourself, you can control the pace of how things should move. Be the master of your craft.

Everybody goes through change. It will either impact you or affect you. Things around you are bound to change. People too will change, and you cannot change that. But you can change the way you see things by changing your attitude toward the change around you. Sometimes change comes to make you better—bitter if you fight it.

Don't fight change; change the fight.

Try as much as you can to pay attention to life, and avoid making simple mistakes. There's a lot to learn from them, but sometimes they are setbacks. I can testify to that. But at the same time, this is how you win. Refuse to set your mind on things that drag you or remind you of your past failures but rather set your mind on the things that will help you learn from the past and to move forward as a better person Drop the baggage, life is full of lessons to learn from.

Chose to remain a student and to earn from every experience you gave. Drop the baggage. Life is full of lessons. Remain a student, and don't be surprised of shortcomings.

When you look at yourself in the mirror, look closely and see the person whom you dream or desire to become. Let the focus of who you are come from within. There's greatness in the inside of you.

"He that believeth on me, as the scripture hath said, out of his belly shall flow rivers of living water" (John 7:38). In you there's greatness. A president, CEO, business owner, entrepreneur, pastor, great musician, architect, and so on. In you is somebody who is going to change the economy of your nation. It's all in you. What do you see when you look at yourself? Choose to see greatness. When you do, God will surprise you with much more that he has in store for you. You will succeed.

You exist because your life carries a distinctive and significant relevance. Never should you ever let yourself think you don't matter. Know why you are in a place you are in and what is the purpose of your existence. God has given you a certain ability, and that makes you capable of execution. When you walk with your ability, God starts to reveal His plan for you. Things are built for performance, and so God created us for a purpose. Walk in all possibilities, for your life is full of capacities. Dare yourself to shift the way you think and get out of your comfort zone.

The steps of a righteous man are ordered by God. Don't think you are moving aimlessly on your own. Whether you slow down or there's quickening, whatever you are going through is just a process. God isn't just preparing a blessing for you, He is preparing you to enjoy your blessing. Your blessing is already prepared. It is written, "Eye hath not seen, nor ear heard, neither have entered into the heart of man, the things which God hath prepared for them that love" (1 Corinthians 2:9).

People may not want to associate with you because they see imperfections in you, but let me tell you something: let them be. God isn't done with you yet. Keep trusting Him. Forget not your closest where you war from (on your knees) and remember to smile, praise and worship God because your confidence is in Him who works in mysterious ways. God is about to set you apart and distinguish you from those who despise you. He is not a respecter of persons. He can bless you beyond those who went before you. Shout amen wherever you are now if you believe. Don't be ashamed of the gospel.

Don't be too hard on yourself. Rather, be real to yourself and appreciate your progress, for where you are today isn't where you were yesterday. Neither is where you are today where you will be tomorrow. But your tomorrow may be today, so prepare and be ready to take the next step. One leads to the other.

I've grown to understand that if you want to enjoy the fruit of your labor, try as much as you can not to live beyond your means as you work out the process to the next level of your finances. Otherwise, every penny you make might end up covering the unexpected spending you incurred in the past. Plan and budget and allow yourself to see your progress. You are blessed and not cursed. Bitten but survived.

You and I were created to worship God. Praise Him in all situations, good or bad. He is God alone. His love for you never changes. I want to remind you that God loves you, and He cares about you. Remind somebody that God loves them.

God's timing is always the best. Regardless of what's going on around you, believe that all things work together for good for them who love God, for them who are called according to His purpose.

There is that time when God remembers you and meets you at your point of need, and He blesses you and makes your heart glad. I pray that God bless you and make you forget your troubles. He is more than able to do exceedingly and abundantly above all you ask. God has endless abilities, and it's for you to enjoy. Have faith in Him.

Find satisfaction in the hope of God's ability. In Him we live, move, and have our being; and He is everything. Your stuff is hidden in the word of God.

Peace comes at a price, but Jesus paid the price. He is the Prince of Peace, and He lives in you. Rest in Him. Rest assured that He has a better plan for you. Situations indicate that God is about to do something in your life. He is a faithful God, and He is about to make you jump and leap for joy.

The harder the battle, the sweeter the victory. When things get hard, go hard too with faith, and trust that God knows your plans. You have to win. You hold many people's hopes. When you win, they win. Remember that God has your back.

Regardless of the turmoil that comes your way, don't ever give up dreaming and believing in yourself. God has your blessing, and it has your name on it. It might take some obstacles and disappointments. When God orders your steps, you don't move aimlessly. Every step you take has meaning. Whatever you are going through is a process. Whatever situation you are in reflects what God is about to do. Praise God in every step you take, whether going front or back. God is saying something to you. May God order your steps to the place of your blessing pain, seemingly wasted time, but you will get it because it's yours. You have to understand that going through such situation is just a fact that it's part of the process.

> "But God, being rich in mercy, because of the great love with which he loved us, even when we were dead in our trespasses, made us alive together with Christ—by grace you have been saved—and raised us up with him and seated us with him in the heavenly places in Christ Jesus, so that in the coming ages he might show the immeasurable riches of his grace in kindness toward us in Christ Jesus" (Ephesians 2:4–7).

The life you choose to live can shape you into the person you always dreamed to be even if nobody was there for you. Rejected, neglected, abandoned—stop the excuses and fight on. God is by your side.

People will never look for who wasn't there for you, but rather, what you have made of yourself. ("God is in me. Shaped by this life.")

You might be living a life that some people are dreaming to live, but if you don't play your cards right and organize yourself, people are going to wake up from their dreams and find you sleepwalking. Arise and walk.

Whatever you spend more time on reflects another side of you and has a lot of impact on your imagery in a perspective on how people around you view you. Build the world around you. Words that run through my mind.

God looks at your destiny even when you fall. He expects you to get up and move forward because you are destined to overcome it. It's in your DNA to succeed. *Thrive*. Let's meet on the other side of success. You belong there.

Regardless of the circumstances, don't give up on yourself. You can still make it. *God is the same yesterday, today, and forever.* He will do it. God's grace is sufficient. In the same way, have faith.

Focus your strength on what you can do best. If you aren't relevant, you are powerless. Stop wasting your time on things that don't matter.

End

About the Author

Solomon is a unique individual who managed to successfully come out of a miserable childhood and background full of rejection, neglect, homelessness, and failure through a positive attitude and mindset in life. He became an influential adult in his community and came to realize that you can deal with an issue all your life. But until you choose to move on with a positive attitude, you will remain stuck in your past, and there's power in a single positive thought. That, in itself, can define your path to recovery. You hold the power to your mind because it's you who feeds it. You hold the switch to a brighter day. Turn it on. He is a mature, patient, peaceful, and intelligent man. He is a problem solver who not only seeks to find solutions to life problems but also empowers others to rise up to be solutions to their community's needs.